Yes, You Can!

You Just Need Help

A Guide to
Personal Accountability

DR. LONNIE E. RILEY

Author of *The Extraordinary Power of 1%*

Yes, You Can!

You Just Need Help

A Guide to
Personal Accountability

DR. LONNIE E. RILEY

Author of *The Extraordinary Power of 1%*

Yes, You Can! You Just Need Help by Dr. Lonnie E. Riley

Published by Freedom Place Publishing

A Division of Freedom Ministries International

Myrtle Beach, SC

www.fmintl.org

Unless otherwise noted, all Scripture quotations are from the New King James Version of the Bible. Copyright © 1979, 1980, 1982 by Thomas Nelson, Inc., publishers.

Cover Design: Kimberly T. Riley

ISBN 9780988445512

Library of Congress Control Number: 2013945545

Printed in the United States of America

Table of Contents

DEDICATION

I can still hear the unmistakable laughter ringing in my memory. I had been on the phone with one of my closest friends and companions of over 35 years discussing my recent book, "_The Extraordinary Power of 1%_". We discussed the process I had gone through, how the sales had gone and I listened as he dreamed of publishing a book as well.

That's when it happened. I told him that I was already working on my next title. "What's this one going to be about, Rile?" He asked. "Accountability" I answered.

"Ha, ha, ha, ha." It rang on for what seemed to be minutes. If it had been anyone else, I might have been offended, but this was David Mercer (affectionately known by me as Merce). Other than my closest family, David knew me better than anyone. He was well aware of my goals, successes, failures and sins.

We had met as schoolmates in the 9th grade. We became roommates for the latter half of that year with another close friend, Todd Hammonds. Merce and I didn't really jell as roommates.

The rest of our time in high school, we became great friends (we didn't room together anymore) and began singing in a gospel quartet with Todd Hammonds and John Neihof. Those were great days and filled our lives with meaning and purpose.

We graduated together and went to the same Bible College. During those days we filled the vacancy of John Neihof in the group with our close friend Tim Wright (later to be David's brother-in-law). As the Crusaders Quartet, we sang often during the school year and spent the summers traveling, singing and preaching together. We recorded our first album while in school.

After graduation from Bible College, we disbanded the group and started our lives independent of one another, so we thought. We did not realize our lives were forever entwined and God would continue to use us to impact each other's future.

David and his wife, Renee, became my pastors during

our early twenties. Daily I would spend time with them and help them as they built a great congregation in the mountains of Kentucky. There David baptized me and dedicated my first born son, Jason Michael Riley.

Merce led me into the Wesleyan Church and helped me as I took my first full-time pastorate in Willard, KY.

We would always minister together. I have preached in his churches and he has preached in mine. We led and served the Wesleyan Youth in Kentucky together. I served as the pastor of his home church and he was on staff at my home church.

For a season, he and I tried to be accountability partners via telephone, but the lack of a face-to-face contact doomed that experiment.

When life was at its hardest for me, he was there. I lost my church, marriage and children (so it seemed at the time), and he was still my friend. He spoke the truth, but always in love. I have always appreciated his forthrightness during those difficult times in my life. When other's decide to talk about me, he spoke to me.

He, along with the rest of the quartet, surprised me when I was in the hospital following my stroke. I was discouraged and unable to walk or talk. Their kind visit was the first time I pulled myself out of bed and we spent hours in the cafeteria laughing and crying together.

We often called each other and bounced ideas off of one another. Sometimes ministers need another minister who has no hidden agenda or who is not part of their staff in whom they can confide. We had that type of relationship.

Now, back to the gut wrenching laughter that started this historical account. Merce knew of my personal failures. He was well acquainted with the lack of accountability that caused it. At first glance, it was amusing to him that I would write on this topic.

Yet as we discussed it further (after he finally stopped laughing), he admitted that from my perspective as one who had failed because of a lack of accountability, I would be the perfect one to focus on its importance. It would be one of the last times I would be privileged to speak to this great man in my life.

I now present this to you, and I humbly dedicate this book to the life and memory of one of my closest friends and accountability partners who over the years has both encouraged and challenged me in my quest to seek after God and to be a man of integrity. You are greatly missed my dear friend! Our next meeting will be around the throne of God as we sing His praises together once again.

In loving memory of

Rev. David Lee (D.L.) Mercer

1961-2012

-xiii-

ACKNOWLEDGEMENTS

Another book has meant more time researching and writing. Early mornings are my favorite time to write, but that can put me on a different sleep schedule from my darling wife, Kim. I am so thankful to her for understanding my writing schedule and quirks. We moved our ministry headquarter to Myrtle Beach, SC and live in a small townhouse. Often I have commandeered the dining room table for all my research and writing. She is such a jewel for putting up with my messes. I could not continue down this path without her love and help. She is talented as a graphic artist and has once again designed the book's cover. Thank you, dear.

On the subject of family, I am also grateful to my children, who have learned the importance of accountability, and seen and experienced the results of a lack of accountability in our family. I love you boys and am daily thankful for your mercy and grace towards me.

Jason Riley and Jeff Mercer have both helped by reading, editing and offering suggestions on content and formatting. Jason took over the technical side and helped with the formatting. Jeff was so kind as to write the foreword and approve of the dedication of the book to his brother, Rev. David L. Mercer.

Special thanks to Renee Mercer, David's wife, and my friend of over 30 years, for allowing me to dedicate the book to his memory. When I asked, you replied in part, "That would mean a lot, Lonnie, if you do that. David was always pulling for you....He believed in you, even when you may have felt as though some didn't." You are often in our thoughts and prayers, Renee, as you raise your family and learn to live without your soul mate by your side each day.

FOREWORD

Dear Reader,

It is my pleasure to recommend this book by Dr. Lonnie Riley, a long-time friend of mine.

By taking on the content of _"Yes, You Can! You Just Need Help!"_ Dr. Riley is in effect challenging a belief many of us hold near and dear to our hearts; a belief that we can and should be furiously independent. In today's culture we prize stoic independent traits and minimize (to the point of near extinction) our natural need for a core support system. By simply describing the benefits of accountability, Dr. Riley masterfully presents a compelling argument otherwise.

With a bit of common sense a person can easily understand that the more minds you have to solve any problem, the more likely we are to succeed. It must be especially true for personal accountability as we are all quite naturally blinded to our own inadequacies. Even if we possess this insight, due to each of our own unique set of rationalizations, we continually repeat the same errors in silent desperation . . . ignoring the support that exists quite naturally around each of us. Dr. Riley shows that by reaching out to others to find an objective accountability partner(s), we can build a much stronger foundation for daily living than we could ever find within ourselves alone.

Whether or not we do so with awareness, each of us already have a support team to surround us and provide for our well-being. Some people that populate our support group fit professional roles: lawyers, accountants, health providers (medical doctors, psychologist, etc.), spiritual leadership, teachers, etc. Other individuals that help us in time of need have a less formal relationship with us: family, friends, neighbors, etc. While we accept these relationships without question, all too many of us neglect the addition of an accountability partner to our support team.

My experiences as a psychologist have left me with no doubt that there is a direct correlation between the mental and spiritual well-being of a person and: 1) the number of their supportive relationships and 2) the quality of the people that make up their support. The attributes of a person's support group will naturally vary from person to person. But the quantity and quality of people one has for friendship and professional support surely has a direct bearing on a person's well-being. Individuals on our support team with poor mental and spiritual hygiene themselves may be worse than no support as they may lead you into poor decisions you may not have made on your own.

Similarly, a high quality of support but not enough of it can also lead to negative results . . . your support team has to have a life of their own as well! It is important to select each member of your team carefully and wisely but nowhere is this truer than with your accountability partner. I highly recommend that you read this accountability tutorial by Dr. Riley and select the type, quantity, and quality of your accountability partner carefully. They may be the most important person on your support team.

I commend you for having the motivation to read Dr. Riley's book and wish you the very best in your endeavors to raise the quality of your life and by default the quality of life for everyone around you.

Jeffery T. Mercer, M.A.

INTRODUCTION

I love being around someone who has a "can do" attitude. I think that nearly everyone loves the energy and excitement that type of person brings into the room. You know who I mean, people who just seem to be able to push through the adversities and challenges of life. They are like the little child's story of the *"Little Engine That Could"* that focused on the "I think I can, I think I can" statements.

Most of us want to be that way. We want to achieve. Grow Spiritually. Meet our own expectations as well as those around us. We desire to keep our commitments and change where we know we can. Too often we fall short. We know deep down that we can do it, but we continually fail.

The good news (Gospel) is that you are right! You CAN do it. You CAN change. You CAN keep your commitments and meet those expectations. You CAN grow spiritually and achieve, *you just need some help*. Enter the topic of accountability.

I remember when I first heard about the topic of personal accountability. I was at a youth leaders training seminar for the southern United States.

The denominational General Secretary of Youth, Keith Drury, and his staff led us for several days, and personal accountability was taught as a part of the personal growth section.

Not long after that meeting, I attended my first Promise Keepers rally. Once again accountability was one of the topics during the meeting. It was one of the promises that the organization was teaching as they toured the country.

Most of us have heard and possibly used the term accountability at work or with our families. We also hear it every election year. Each political party says that we must hold the other accountable for their votes, decisions and actions since their election.

The subject of a personal accountability relationship is one often spoken of by ministers today. This is the voluntarily relationship where people help each other become more dedicated to fulfilling their goals and stated commitments. Having been in some type of ministry for over thirty years, I have seen how the topic has grown in popularity and in some form changed in implementation (though not always effective, hence this book).

Though the message sounds reasonable, too often there is no practical side to it. No nuts and bolts guiding us or telling us how to go about the accountability process. It is not the minister's fault, as they often do not really know themselves.

The truth is, they may not have a vibrant personal accountability relationship. I know I did not.

I tried for years to have an accountability partner. I went through them like crazy. At one point one of my best friends (David Mercer) who was also a pastor and I tried to hold each other accountable over the phone. We both learned that long distance accountability is nearly impossible to maintain with any measure of authenticity. At another point I had an older, seasoned man in one of my churches hold me accountable for certain professional aspects of my ministry. This was fairly effective, but it evolved into more of a "father and son" relationship and lost some of its teeth.

Next I entered into an accountability relationship with another pastor in the area. We had our relationship as friends and tried to move into accountability, and the hard-hitting questions were not asked on a consistent basis. Eventually we both fell and failed in our ministry and marriages. People were hurt and our lives devastated. Perhaps all of that would have been saved if we had known how to walk in real accountability.

My prayer for you as you read this book is that you will find practical information and guidelines that will protect you and your family. In providing this knowledge, I hope to assist in making you a stronger man or woman for God.

Believing you can do it,
Dr. Lonnie E. Riley

SURE,
NO PROBLEM

CHAPTER 1

"The righteous man walks in his integrity;
His children are blessed after him"
Proverbs 20:7

D o you want one? Nearly every day either I want one, or someone wants one from me. It seems as though everyone wants one. We feel constantly approached from every area, aspect and stage of life by people asking, seeking and knocking for one.

"Sure, No Problem!" is too often our response. What is it they want from us?

A COMMITMENT

When we make a commitment, it means that we have pledged to do something. We have given our word. When we give our word, our integrity is at stake.

YES, YOU CAN! YOU JUST NEED HELP

You know the old saying, "My word is my bond?" Well, that is only valid if there is strength or unity behind your words. The validity of our testimony or walk with God and our fellow man is based upon our integrity.

Each commitment we make has the potential of either building up or tearing down our personal integrity. Have you ever commented that someone you know, "Says what he means and means what he says"? What you are basically saying is that they are a person of integrity. You have determined that because the person has proven faithful to the commitments they have made in the past.

> **When we make a commitment, it means that we have pledged to do something.**

The Scriptures have placed importance on a person walking in integrity.

Take Proverbs 20:7 for example,

"The righteous man walks in his
integrity; His children are blessed after him."

David, though he sinned, was able to describe himself as one who would walk in integrity. Psalm 26:11,

"But as for me, I will walk in my integrity;
Redeem me and be merciful to me."

MEET TOM

Different people desire varying levels of commitment from us, but a commitment none the less. Consider "Tom." He is a likable guy who is trying his best to build a nice life for his family.

He has a supportive wife and 2 great kids. He's had the same job for the last ten years and lives in a moderate, middle class neighborhood. Most importantly, Tom is a Christian man. He goes to church every week, puts money in the offering, and only listens to Christian music on the radio.

He desires to make a lasting difference in the areas of his life where God has placed him. He wants to be known as a man of his word and one who walks in integrity. Let's take a quick look at one possible week in Tom's life.

SUNDAY

Church is awesome. The pastor announces that the youth group needs someone to assist the youth pastor. Tom has always enjoyed being around kids and thinks of what his life could have been like if he had only known about Jesus at that age. Filled with a burden and hoping to make a difference, Tom catches the youth pastor after church and volunteers to be his helper.

The youth pastor explains that the time commitment is Sunday evening youth service, Tuesday evening planning meeting, Wednesday evening Bible study and Saturday events and fundraisers. Tom is ecstatic at the possibilities and says he will "make it work."

The rest of day is filled with lunch at the Chinese buffet and a couple of football games. His mind continues to wander toward the youth ministry at the church and he silently prays several times during the day that God will use him in a dramatic and meaningful way in the lives of these teenagers. "Just one!" He keeps thinking. "If I can influence just one of the kids for God, it will be worth it!"

Tom's wife has rarely seen him so excited, especially concerning his involvement at the church. Her heart is comforted as she sees Tom pushing beyond his comfort zone by reaching out to these teenagers. She is proud of Tom and lets him know it.

MONDAY

It's just like any other beginning to the work week. Tom is trying hard to focus his mind, but the new position with youth is burning inside his spirit. Right after lunch, Tom's boss calls a meeting. The boss is so excited he can hardly contain himself. He announces that they have the opportunity to pick up the account of their dreams.

This would turn the company from a simple mid-sized organization into a real player in the industry. Many new people will have to be hired and trained to meet the demands. However, until the deal is solidified, everyone is expected to give 110%.

Of course, the boss announces, this means working late and preparing for the new increase in sales and production. Instead of closing at 5:00, everyone is expected to stay until the job is done each day. "No later than 7:00," he promises.

Everyone in the company (including Tom) is excited and is willing to make the additional sacrifices necessary to expand the business. The potential is evident and the enthusiasm is racing through the offices like wild-fire.

Tom gets home and tells his wife all about the new account and the possibilities for the company and perhaps even a place for him to expand his leadership and also get a promotion and a raise. She shares his excitement and can see the opportunities this can open up for their family.

Her only reservation is the time Tom must take away from their family, especially in light of the new position he has taken with the youth program at church. Tom reassures her of his ability and competence. "I can do this" he tells her." She promises to support him and help him when she can. She is well aware of the time and commitment this decision will cost, for everyone in the family.

TUESDAY

Tom's boss calls him into a private meeting. Because of his experience and time on the job, Tom has been selected to develop a training program for all the new hires. This promotes him to vice-president of training, which means a hefty salary and benefits increase.

"Wow," Tom thought, "I can't believe my blessings. I was just obedient to answer the call for help at church and now God blesses me with this new position." Tom moves into his new corner office with a great view of the park and begins on the training manual right away. "It will require a lot of time and effort, but it will be worth it in the end," Tom dreams. "Who knows, if everything goes right I could be the president of the company someday."

That evening, he and his wife bow their heads and thank God for opening these wonderful doors of ministry and provision.

WEDNESDAY

First thing that morning Tom receives a phone call from the youth pastor at the church. "We missed you at the planning meeting last night Tom," the youth pastor says. "Wow, I totally forgot," Tom explains, "I was just promoted to VP yesterday and I have a lot of my plate now and it just skipped my mind. I'm sorry. It'll never happen again. I'm entering it into my smart phone right now."

The youth pastor totally understands and tells Tom not to worry about it. "Don't forget the Bible study tonight," he reminds Tom. "I'll be there with bells on!" Tom responds.

Tom's day is now filled with meetings with human resources and the hiring manager. Everyone has some fantastic ideas and Tom is riding on enthusiasm and hype. When one of his assistants says she has to leave,

YES, YOU CAN! YOU JUST NEED HELP

Tom realizes that it is already 7:00. He jumps in his car and heads to church. "Better late than never," he thinks. He makes it for the last part of the youth Bible study.

What a great study it was! Tom enjoyed hearing the kids give their testimonies and to hear them pray for one another really touched his heart. "This is exactly what I need to be doing," he told another volunteer.

After the study, Tom jumps into his old Ford and it won't start. Thankfully one of the mechanics that attend the church was there for another meeting and was able to help him get it started. "You have a real problem here, Tom," the mechanic shared. "You're probably going to have to put some real money into this machine to bring it up to speed."

Tom finally arrives at home and tells his wife everything over a cold dinner. She's excited too. Tom stays up later to write down some training ideas as his wife and kids go on to bed. Sleep doesn't come easy as his mind is running at top speed and the future looks brighter than he has ever envisioned it to be. He also begins to think that with his new position, he will be able to help fund some youth events.

THURSDAY

It's a full day. It goes by so fast when you are enjoying what you are doing. Meetings, planning, dreaming and writing fill up his day until he looks out his window and realizes that it's dark. Way past 7:00. "What a great productive day this was," Tom thinks. "I guess I should call it a night and head home."

He squints as he tries the ignition on his Ford. Yes! It started. Home he goes, only to arrive and find that both of his boys are asleep and his wife was just going to bed.

"Be patient, it will pass soon," he tells her as she mumbles something under her breath and turns her head toward the wall.

FRIDAY

It is the end of an exciting and fulfilling week. Tom accomplished so much, but there is still a lot to be done. He finishes the outline for the training manual and presents it to his boss.

It wasn't a very good meeting. The boss is stressing out over the deadlines the new account has placed on him. He makes a few adjustments to Tom's outline and then proceeds to ask Tom to carry a "little more" responsibility for the next month or so. Tom sees the potential and rises to the occasion. He loves feeling needed by his company.

Time gets away from him again and he realizes that he will not have the time to take his wife out for their weekly date. She understands when he calls, and cancels the baby-sitter. "I'll make it up to you, sweetheart," Tom promises.

SATURDAY

Tom rises early in order to take his sons to baseball tryouts. One is in T-ball and the other in the coach-pitch league. All morning, between jotting down ideas for his meetings at work next week, Tom watches as his boys exhibit their skills (or lack of the same) and promises each of them that he will work on their batting and catching so they can earn a starting position on the team.

After baseball, Tom takes the kids with him to a car dealership. He spends all afternoon negotiating the price of a new luxury sedan.

"I can afford it," he justifies, "My new raise will more than cover the payment." After several hours, he takes his kids home and surprises his wife with a brand new vehicle.

YES, YOU CAN! YOU JUST NEED HELP

While showing his new car to his neighbor, Tom is interrupted by a gentleman in a suit. This man introduces himself as a local life insurance salesman and asks Tom for a few minutes of his time in order to review Tom's coverage. Tom agrees and is astonished at what the insurance man reveals. Considering Tom's debts, living expenses, college goals for his boys, and possible unexpected health problems, he is extremely under-insured. If something where to happen to Tom, he wanted to make sure that his family was able to survive and thrive during the months and years following.

Tom agrees with the salesman and signs the new policy, committing to a new monthly payment in order to cover his life and protect his family.

Tom feels good after all of the transactions of the day. "Let's all go out and celebrate," he says. So they dress up and splurge on a fancy dinner to rejoice in their new blessings from God.

"Oops," Tom replies to the youth pastor when he calls. "I just had an incredibly busy day and honestly forgot about the youth car wash. Be patient with me as I try to shuffle all the new things on my plate," he adds. Full of grace the youth pastor understands, encourages and celebrates with Tom.

As you can tell, Tom is good hearted, hardworking and loves providing for his family. The problem is that his good intentions can quickly cause him to be overloaded. His "burning desire" can lead to "burn out."

A WORLD
FULL OF TOMS

Can you relate to Tom? I know I can. I have both felt and allowed myself to succumb to the pressures of life. The Scriptures command us to *"not let the world squeeze you into its mold*" (Romans 12:2) yet most of us have done exactly that.

"You deserve it," they say. "Wear this and you will be cool, drive one of these and you will appear successful, live here and you will be recognized as someone who has made it to the top." And you can have it all by committing your time, abilities, money, emotions and it feels like even your soul to them.

> **It is with good intentions that we make those commitments**

It is with good intentions that we make those commitments. Often it is because we do not want to turn someone down, disappoint those we love, or have anyone's confidence in us diminished.

As parents, we raise our hands during the close of a church service "committing" to spend more time with our children. We walk a church aisle and take the hand of our chosen mate and make the "commitment" to love, honor and cherish until death do us part.

We sign on the dotted line and commit to make those "easy" monthly payments. We bow our heads in prayer and make a "commitment" of our lives to Christ. Year after year we "resolve" that in the New Year we will pray more, spend less, reduce debt, lose weight, spend more time at home and less at work, and witness more for Jesus.

In America we have romanticized the notion that we can do everything and create our own fortunes ourselves. We are the "John Waynes" of the world and nothing is too difficult for us. We have the intestinal fortitude to push through all difficulties and challenges, rising above them all in the end as the master of our future and the architect of our fate.

Our society has given accolades to those who can effectively multi-task in every area of their lives.

Hollywood has almost created a third dimension in which people live an alternate life. Often they think they can act just like the actors and actresses in their favorite movie or television show and that things will work out in their life just as it does in the script.

Even as a pastor I recall thinking that I could do everything myself. I can personally remember going to a church growth conference and hearing a stirring message on personal soul winning. Hundreds of us stood to our feet, moved by the dramatic presentation. We all made a public commitment to be more of an outgoing and purposeful evangelist for Jesus Christ.

It seems that nearly everyone wants us to make some level of commitment to them or their cause. And guess what, making the commitment is easy.

SO, WHAT'S THE PROBLEM?

CHAPTER 2

"Jesus replied, 'No one who puts his hand to the plow and looks back is fit for service in the kingdom of God."

Luke 9:62

The real problem we, and all the other "Toms" in the world face, is not making commitments . . . . but **KEEPING THEM.**

When we make these commitments, our intentions are honorable, and our motives may be pure. Our desire to do the right thing and to become a better person is scripturally sound.

Boldly, we answer the call of God to change habits that are destroying our lives. The problem is, we often fail.

Perhaps we do well for a while. Sincerely wanting to be known as a man or woman of our word, we try to hold steady. In an effort, to protect our integrity, we persevere. We hold our heads up high, as we should, and feel the joy of victory.

Almost predictably, however, when pressures mount, and schedules fill, we become weak and grow slack in our resolve. Then, in a moment of strong temptation or over-confidence, we lack the fortitude to keep our demanding commitments and we fail.

> **The real problem is not making commitments . . . . . but KEEPING THEM.**

Once we have failed, we rarely have the inner strength to get up and keep trying. More often than not, when we fail, we throw our hands up in surrender and quit.

TOM'S PROBLEM

Let's talk about "Tom" again. Though he has tried time and again to keep the myriad of commitments he has made over the years, he just keeps failing.

Work, family, marriage and church are all pulling at him from what seems like a thousand different angles. One commitment always overlaps the other. Time is in short demand and Tom is beginning to feel the pressure. He's always trying to shuffle between his family, church, and work.

> **We become weak and grow slack on our resolve.**

The "big account" fell through, so he lost his big promotion and the pay that went with it. Now he's constantly robbing from Peter to pay Paul in order to keep his car and his life insurance.

What can he do? Where do you go for the answers?
What are all the questions? One can almost hear him
thinking, "God blessed me and now I can't keep up,
what's up with that?"

Remembering advice from one of his pastor's
sermons, Tom begins to search the Bible for answers to
his dilemma. Then, early one morning during his
devotional time, he comes across a verse in the Old
Testament that jumps off the page at him and instead of
leaving his private time with God encouraged, he is
discouraged and wonders, "What's the use." What kind
of verse would do that to him? His little devotional had
led him to Ecclesiastes 5:4-5,

> *"When you make a vow to God, do not delay*
> *in fulfilling it. He has no pleasure in fools;*
> *fulfill your vow. It is better not to vow than*
> *to make avow and not fulfill it."*

He lays down his Bible, pen and pad and just stares into space. "I'm a failure," he says to himself. "I can't have the pleasure of God on my life. I'm a fool like the verse says. I'll never be able to change my life."

So, Tom abandons his personal prayer time and **opts to watch** a television preacher. Who knew that the televangelist would be lifting Luke 9:62 out as his text?

"Jesus replied, 'No one who puts his hand to the plow and looks back is fit for service in the kingdom of God.'"

Ouch! These words just bring more guilt and tend to load on the

> **It is better not to vow than to make a vow and not fulfill it.**

condemnation. Not only has Tom disappointed his family, employer, creditors, or church, he has also broken a vow before Almighty God and turned back from the things he laid his hands to do. Whew, that's heavy stuff.

<u>OUR PROBLEM</u>

We go through the same feelings. Maybe we don't read that verse or hear some preacher say it, but we know it deep in our hearts and it eats away at us.

Then, even though there are all these negative feelings, we tend to continue to make more commitments in the hopes that maybe we can keep the next one. So the cycle continues.

> **We can all look in the mirror of our lives and see the reflection of un-kept commitments**

Especially in this "easy pay" age, when consumer debt is climbing, and the inability to meet those financial commitments is forcing many families into bankruptcy.

SO, WHAT'S THE PROBLEM?

The pressure of these financial commitments is testing the foundation of marital relationships and many are found weak at best and defective at worst. Financial problems are often stated as a primary reason for divorce. Since the most common financial difficulty is debt, we can see where our inability to keep those "easy pay" commitments affects our lives.

We can all look in the mirror of our lives and see the reflection of un-kept commitments. We have all fallen into the pit of failure and felt the agony of defeat. We recognize that we readily make commitments and then struggle to keep them.

Think about the loans you have signed for. It's pretty easy to agree to make those payments, but it is a totally different story once the "new" has worn off of the item (car, TV, furniture, etc.). That's when making those payments can become a chore and when all of life begins to demand more money, it can be easy to let a payment slide or, even worse, pay it with a credit card and begin the vicious cycle all over again. That just creates more debt and another commitment to keep.

CHURCH

> **. . . we readily make commitments and then struggle to keep them.**

What about your commitments to your church? Have you told others that you will get involved in a certain ministry, but failed to do it? As a pastor I have had this happen often. I've had people say they are excited about beginning a phone ministry, a care ministry, a soul-winning ministry, or a greeter ministry. They have promised to put together a church directory, a prayer chain or even something as simple as a church cleaning schedule. They have told me they want to play an instrument on the worship team or be a vocalist there.

I have been a pastor long enough to see most every type of promise made to me or the church and watched well-meaning, faith-filled, saved, and sanctified people drop the ball. They make the commitment, but don't follow through with it.

Then there is our commitment to God. I hope you realize that your church commitments and your promises to God are not always the same.

Remember the story I told you about the evangelism conference? The sad news is that my new found "fire" was soon extinguished. Though I knew the biblical call to witness, I was not motivated to make the effort to go soul winning. The excitement of the moment wore off and I was left looking at a commitment card that I had signed.

The humbling truth is that I allowed other things to become more important, and the long list of other commitments to make demands on my time. I always intended to get around to it, but never did.   As a result of this procrastination, I found myself at the same conference the next year under a load of guilt because I had not kept my promise. When the speaker asked for those who had been faithful to their promise to stand, I just shrunk down into my chair and hid behind the guy seated in front of me. I was ashamed.

GOOD NEWS

I have some really good news for you; recognizing a pattern of defeat is often the first step in applying the remedy. Knowing that we have placed too many irons in the fire is the initial move toward a more consistent life of keeping our word.   "My word is my bond" can once again ring true in our inner man.

The Thrill Of Victory Or The Agony Of Defeat?

CHAPTER 3

"Simon Peter said to them, 'I am going fishing.'
They said to him, 'We are going with you also.'
They went out and immediately got into the boat,
and that night they caught nothing."

John 21:3

A life of victory or a life of defeat is often the result of a cycle of the same. The person who lives a defeated life is one who has continually been defeated and then assumes an attitude of defeatism. Thus it becomes true that our attitude determines our performance.

If we sow a defeatist attitude, we will reap a lifestyle and life-pattern of defeat. It will become a cycle. We will find ourselves caught in the downward funnel of defeat and soon become content with it in our lives.

Commitments will become little more than just a

meaningless public display with no real intent to keep them. Our word will have little meaning and our self-esteem will diminish. We become what we say we hate, "A Hypocrite."

The life of victory is also the result of a cycle. A life of victory is a life of optimistic possibility. An attitude of perseverance or "not willing to give up" will more likely lead to success, achievement, and accomplishment.

> **A life of victory or a life of defeat is often the result of a cycle of the same.**

Once we have experienced victory in certain areas of our life, then we have a solid foundation on which to face the next area(s) of our life. Each victory adds another brick and we can stand firm in the face of the challenges.

REVISITING TOM

Let's see how this principle worked in Tom's life. As everything was working in Tom's favor, he was thrilled and exhilarated at the possibilities. He was working harder and achieving more than he ever thought he would.

Then he began to make decisions based on emotion and found himself buried under a load of responsibilities that were too heavy for him to bear. Once he began to miss meetings and have to reschedule events in his life,

> **We become what we say we hate, "A Hypocrite."**

he took on a defeatist attitude and the "blessings" quickly became the source of his disappointment. He no longer possessed positive emotions about his decisions and commitments. This is often the case when emotions are the ruling factor in making those decisions and commitments.

Tom decides that his commitment level is not the problem, but that he has allowed other things to crowd his love and passion for God out of his life. "I'm going to get serious about my Christian duty," he thinks. The next church service he renews his dedication to God and His purpose for his life. He walks the aisle at church and confesses his "idolatry" and promises everyone that he will be a different man.

He's excited again. "Maybe I need something in my life to keep me focused on my promises and yet allow me to get closer to God as well," he tells his wife. So after the youth meetings, Tom speaks with the Senior Pastor about beginning a men's group that studies responsibility and ways to assist them with time management. The pastor give Tom permission and with a new vigor Tom creates extra time in his calendar. An hour of two for the meeting each week, as well as several hours of reading and studying to present each meeting should suffice.

ON A POSITIVE NOTE

As a teenager, I began showing interest in singing at my Christian high school. I worked with three others to form a male quartet. We worked hard and practiced long for our first performance. I was terrified at the thought of singing in front of hundreds of people that I knew. What if I got off key or was too loud or too soft. I literally thought that I was going to make myself sick.

> **Each victory adds another brick and we can stand firm in the face of the challenges**

The day came for the performance, and as we stood tall together, we did the best job we could. I felt exhilarated. I was so excited. I just knew that if I could sing here that it was only a matter of time before I would be singing other places. And that mental attitude brought about by a victory proved to be prophetic. I traveled three summers singing in different churches all over the U.S. and Canada. Since then I have made a total of 5 recordings and performed in front of thousands. Now I write music and play and sing every week in church. I have lead music in 4 different churches over my career. That one victory has changed my life.

> ... it will create a victorious life

As we push ourselves to experience victory in the matter of our commitments, we do so with a hope that we will establish a pattern of victory. This will then fuel us for victory in the next challenging commitment. A transforming cycle will begin to form and it will create a victorious life, a joyful and a meaningful life. This does not mean that God loves you more because you have kept your commitments; it means you have shown your love for God as you have allowed Jesus to live through you in a spirit of integrity and truth.

WHAT'S THE USE?

Those of us, who find that we are continually making promises that are never kept, or cannot be kept, can fall victim to a swing of the pendulum the other way. We over react and make a different type of negative commitment, one that I call;

The "No Commitment Syndrome"

Or another way of putting it is we just decide, "What's the use?" or "Why try?"

Because we have been living in a cycle of defeat, we can become so discouraged that we choose to avoid the experiences of failure. How can we avoid experiencing the failure to keep commitments? Often the answer is by ceasing to make meaningful commitments.

Thus the, "No Commitment Syndrome." We reason like this; "You can't fail if you haven't tried." "You cannot be disappointed if you haven't put forth the effort." It's an easy way out, and often we decide to take the path of least resistance.

> **Often we decide to take the path of least resistance**

DOUBTING TOM

Let's revisit our buddy Tom. Because he has failed in the past with other kinds of commitments, he decides to avoid the negative feelings of failing by making the internal , mental decision to make no more commitments.

Now, when the Spirit of God is speaking to him in church, he avoids that trip to an altar of prayer. He also chooses to run away from the challenge to live a pure life. He refuses to sign a pledge card to become a man of prayer. He decides not to stand in order to promise to have regular devotions.

What's the use, or Why Try?

Since he could not change before, he avoids confronting his pornography habit. He stops worrying about trying to become a better husband or father. He just stops making commitments all together because, "What's the use, I'll just fail anyway," has become his slogan. His theme song is now like a country and western ballad describingthe hurts of the past instead of a victorious battle march claiming the possession of new territory.

WHY TRY

Have you been there with Tom? The horror of this attitude is that we become content with mediocrity and grow accustomed to living with less than God's best in our life. We accept the fact that we have failed before and assume that we will always fail to keep our word.

There are too many Christians today not really plugged into their place in the church. They are not making a positive difference because of past failures that have led to unwillingness to risk trying anything further. There are even ministers who have failed or fallen and have allowed their past to dictate their future rather than God's forgiveness.

Still, looming in the caverns of our mind is the real desire to become that man or woman of integrity. We can never really run from it, we just appease it by making empty commitments, or by suppressing it.

VICTORY OR DEFEAT?

The answer is NOT to stop making commitments, but rather to find a way to honestly keep those commitments that we have made. We must find a tool, something that will motivate us, that will help keep us true to our word and encourage us to overcome the weaknesses in our lives.

WHAT CAN I DO?

CHAPTER 4

"As iron sharpens iron, so one man sharpens another."

Proverbs 27:17

H aving identified this dragon of a problem that has held so many captive, let us examine a very successful solution dressed in the armor of "Accountability." This is one element that is usually consistently missing in the battle for a commitment-keeping life.

Accountability is in its most basic form a math or bookkeeping term. In that context, it means to keep a record or an account of the income and expenses of a business or person in order to keep them in balance. The goal is to understand where money comes from and where it goes. In this way, one can increase the income and decrease the expenses and show ways to help the business have a greater financial worth.

When applied to the context in which we are using it, accountability carries a similar meaning. It is having someone who checks our progress toward keeping our commitments. Someone we answer to for those commitments we have made. A person who gives both encouragement and reproof as needed.

> **Having someone who checks our progress**

Basically, they are an "accountant" that sees whether or not our life is kept in balance and where we can increase or decrease effort to make our life have a greater sense of worth or meaning.

We may not realize it, but we have been accustomed to accountability most of our lives. It has been built into our daily processes and helped develop us to this point.

IT WORKS AT WORK

Stephen Covey in his book, *"The Seven Habits of Highly Effective People,"* rates accountability as extremely important to getting the job properly done in a corporate setting.

For example, a manager will keep employees accountable for the accomplishment of certain tasks because they know that he is watching both them and the clock

MBWA

and they are more likely to perform as expected. If the manager never checks progress, or the employee's work time, then their work output will diminish. That is simple, structured accountability.

Peter Drucker called it, "MBWA" or Management By Wondering Around. In his studies he found that a manager who sat in his office most of the time having meetings and doing paper work would have less productive employees than the manager who merely walked around the plant. Why? Because the employees knew the manager was walking around the plant and could be watching them at anytime, they didn't goof off since they might be seen and possibly lose their job. They were being held accountable.

IT WORKED IN SCHOOL

I first experienced this type of response when I was in elementary school. At the end of a chapter or section, the teacher would give us a test that covered the material. As I think back on those days, I remember that if the teacher walked around the room, looking at our work as we took the test there were fewer incidences of cheating than when the teacher just sat at her desk and worked while the kids took the test. Accountability was at work.

I'M AN EXCELLENT DRIVER!

Do you remember that line from the movie, "*Rain Man*?" This principle hits me every now and then while driving. I am a safe driver. I have never had a speeding ticket nor been in a major accident. But if I look in the rearview mirror while driving and see a police car behind me, I automatically check my speed and adjust if necessary.

As long as the officer is there I feel nervous. I make sure I use my turn signal for everything. I don't follow other cars too closely. I obey all the rules of the road. I become the perfect driver. As soon as the police cruiser turns another direction or passes me, I take a deep breath of relief and can wipe my sweaty palms.

That's accountability at work. Come on. You've experienced that to. Honesty is necessary for success too you know. You may as well admit it.

FIGHTING CRIME

I recently attended a neighborhood watch meeting. It was lead by a local policeman. He said that this group (59 of us that night) had helped clean up our area of town to the tune of 20 arrests in the past month. The police department expects that crime in our area will drop significantly as word gets out that there are all of these people watching everything that is going on in our neighborhood. In others words, once the criminals realize that they will be held accountable for their actions in our part of town, they will move to another section of the city.

IT WILL WORK FOR YOU!

As Christians, we should always be aware that our Lord is watching every move we make. He is keeping an eye on our progress. But far too often we fall into the trap of "out of sight, out of mind" and since we don't see God with our physical eye, we choose, consciously or subconsciously, to not remember He is there.

So, for more practical purposes, our desire to live a godly life could better be achieved if we developed an accountability relationship with a fellow believer. Having someone to check our progress and "hold our feet to the flame," on the important issues of our lives can help keep us on target.

We fall into the trap of "out of sight, out of mind"

If we have to be responsible to, answer to, or give an explanation for our actions, perhaps our actions will change. Do you remember the beating of Rodney King? The police were videotaped and that tape was handed over to the authorities. These men were then held accountable for their actions. If they had known they were being videotaped, their actions would no doubt have been quite different. So it is with us in our lives. Hey, if we were followed around all day by someone with a video camera, would our actions change?

IT IS BIBLICAL

In a Christian setting, this accountability is believer to believer. It is a very personal relationship and based on biblical principles.

Verses such as Proverbs 27:17,

> *"As iron sharpens iron, so one man sharpens another."*

and Ecclesiastes 4:9-12,

> *"Two are better than one; because they have a good return for their work: If one falls down, his friend can help him up!*

Also, if two lie down together, they will keep warm. But how can one keep warm alone? Though one may be overpowered, two can defend themselves. A cord of three strands is not quickly broken"

illustrate some of the biblical background of accountability.

God's word in the New Testament in particular is clear that we are to be a body that is in relationship with one another.

MEASURE YOUR LIFE

Gene A. Getz in his landmark book, *The Measure Of A Man,* makes a strong case for men to have an accountability relationship with another man. He states, "Every Christian man should have another Christian man as an accountability partner. Having an accountability partner has become more and more necessary in the culture in which we live."

He defines his view of this relationship as, "An accountability partner is another man who helps each of us to keep from yielding to temptation, and when we do yield, to help us experience forgiveness and not to repeat the sinful action."

He goes on to offer a list of possible accountability questions the men of his church are encouraged to use. The following ten questions are introspective as well as effective:

How often did you meet with God this week?

What has God been saying to you through His Word this week?

What sins in your personal or business life did you experience this week that need confession?

WHAT CAN I DO?

Are you giving to the Lord's work regularly and proportionately as God has blessed you? What percentage did you give last month?

What movies did you see this past week? Do you feel good about viewing these movies? Would you be able to tell your fellow Christians in your church what you have seen without being embarrassed?

How did you influence your marriage and family this week? How positively? How negatively? What could you do to improve?

Did you pray for me/us this week?

What challenges or struggles are weighing on your mind?

What lives did you influence for Christ this week?

YES, YOU CAN! YOU JUST NEED HELP

Did you just lie to me?

Dr. Getz is recommending a personal accountability between men. There are many different types and levels of accountability. We each must evaluate the strengths and weaknesses of each particular type and decide which will fit best into their life. Though there may be many, we will discuss five in the coming chapters: Mentor, Group, Couple, Spousal and Mutual/One-on-one.

MENTOR

CHAPTER 5

"For this reason I have sent Timothy to you, who is my beloved and faithful son in the Lord, who will remind you of my ways in Christ, as I teach everywhere in every church."

1 Corinthians 4:17

One means of establishing accountability is a mentor/mentee relationship. This entails making ourselves accountable to someone who is an older or a more mature Christian than us. The younger, or newer, Christian is held accountable by the more mature Christian.

In this method, however the older person is not being held accountable by the younger. This "one-way" accountability can be very beneficial and help newer Christians secure a solid foundation from the shared experiences and instruction of spiritual leaders.

This type of relationship can be seen throughout the Scriptures.

JOSHUA

Joshua was a young man when Israel was delivered from slavery in Egypt. Though he had lived as a slave, probably working in Pharaoh's brick yards, I believe he dreamed of being and doing more. He, like all of us, had untapped potential. Though a diamond in the rough, he had a gift of leadership. He was full of raw potential, but he needed some shaping. That's where God used Moses in Joshua's life. He was mentored by Moses.

> He dreamed of being and doing more.

Over his life, Joshua had several different connections with his mentor. He was Moses' servant, he was chosen as one of the 12 spies that infiltrated the Promised Land, and he was the general of Israel's army. Though he didn't emulate Moses' life or become a clone, he followed Moses' example and eventually became the next leader of the nation of Israel.

He watched as Moses met God on the mountain. We see in Exodus 33 that he would follow Moses to the tent of meeting and stay outside while Moses met with God. God's glory would fill the tent and Moses would receive direction, strength and encouragement.

> He developed a love for the presence of God by following Moses.

Once Moses left the tent, Joshua would stay and bask in the glory of God that remained. He developed a love for the presence of God by following Moses. His 40 years of serving Moses and the people of Israel prepared him to become the next leader .

ELISHA

Elisha followed Elijah as a prophet in Israel. God put the two of them together for a season. Why? I believe because Elisha needed the mentoring of Elijah before he was ready to step into the national spotlight. Elijah had been a mighty man of God. He had performed many miracles that had never been seen or heard of in Israel before. Elijah had secured a great win over the prophets of Baal at Mount Carmel. Yet, in order for God's purpose in the nation to be advanced, another strong leader needed to emerge.

Elisha desired to be used by God. Certainly the rebellious nation of Israel could use some Godly guidance. He believed in the power of God and the office of a prophet. He was full of untapped potential and he knew the necessity of the anointing of the Holy Spirit.

The relationship these two men had, developed in Elisha a deep longing to walk in that type of life changing power. When Elijah was taken to heaven, Elisha was there and his request of a double portion of Elijah's spiritual power was granted to him. He then went on to become Israel's next great prophet. He served Elijah well, and learned the office of prophet by submitting himself to God's man for a season.

> **He learned the office of prophet by submitting himself to God's man for a season.**

TIMOTHY

Timothy was an up and coming young man in the Church of the New Testament. As a young man, I believe Timothy knew that God had a plan and purpose for his life. Like his mother and grandmother, he had come to faith in Jesus and was filled with the Holy Spirit of God. His gifts and passions helped him realize that God was calling him to full time ministry to a world that had not yet learned or even heard of Jesus Christ.

The Apostle Paul became his mentor. Paul took Timothy with him as he traveled through the gentile regions and proclaimed the Gospel. Timothy watched Paul, not only as he ministered and taught before the crowds, but also he watched Paul's daily walk with Jesus.

He observed how Paul prayed. He listened as Paul spoke of God's direction and call on their lives. He learned how to stand up for the truth and he cultivated the selfless attitude he saw Paul exhibit when placed in prison or beaten.

Paul wrote two letters to Timothy in the New Testament and even referenced their "father/son" relationship several times in Holy Scripture. Even then Paul was encouraging and teaching Timothy, mentoring him from a distance.

JESUS AND THE DISCIPLES

The ultimate mentor relationship in the Bible is Jesus and His disciples. The term "disciple" has been watered down over the years to just mean the twelve apostles who followed Jesus and inherited His church. The true meaning of discipleship in Jesus' time was actually a mentoring relationship.

> **The Disciples learned everything from Jesus**

They learned everything from Him: how to pray, how to preach, how to cast out demons, how to fast, how to stand when the truth is not popular with the religious establishment, how to relate with each other, how to love the sinner, how to submit to God, how to serve others, how to deal with betrayal, how to lay down your life for your friends and calling. And they learned it well.

The final command of Jesus to His disciples, known to us as the great commission, was to continue this mentoring relationship. He tells His followers to go into the entire world and "make disciples."

Those early church leaders did just that and began a process of mentoring others as the young church expanded across the globe as Jesus commanded.

MENTORING
IN SOCIETY

Mentoring has caught on even in the corporate world. As I received my licenses to sell stocks and bonds, the company I was working for assigned a mentor to me. His responsibility was to ensure that I understood the company policies and procedures as well as to aid me in my success. He had his own successful branch and I was expected to learn from his experiences as I prepared to open my own office. I went into his office every day and worked for and with him. I learned the way the company expected for me to answer the phone, place orders, deal with customers, attack problems and file reports.

Many social programs have adapted the mentoring model for their system. I can recall the big brother program that placed an older male with younger children as a mentor. The "big brother" is more than just a friend to the child; they are there to instill values and ethics that may be lacking in the fatherless child's life. The program has been a great success over the years, developing children into productive young men in our society. Great stories abound of the kids rising above poverty, abuse and addiction to become great leaders.

> **The mentor should be a person we respect**

Most recently I joined a business networking group. It is an international national group and has had tremendous success is generating referrals for its members. Once you have applied for membership, paid your dues, and have been inducted as a member in the local chapter, the next step is that you are assigned a mentor to walk you through your first 6 weeks as a member.

Many churches these days offer mentoring programs in specific areas of ministry. Leaders like John Maxwell have dedicated their lives by focusing on the development of true leadership.

FIND A MENTOR

In seeking a mentor, we should be sure to know that they have been victorious in the areas that we need the most accountability. The mentor should also be a person whom we respect and would feel the effect of letting them down. We must be willing to submit to their judgment and authority.

Mentoring, or one way accountability, can have it weaknesses. It is hard to have someone always telling you what to do or checking up on you. This can be exasperated, if you are not sure if they are victorious or at least accountable to someone else.

Mentoring may be best suited for developing oneself in a particular area that the mentor has expertise in. At times it can be very difficult when it comes to sharing the intimate details of our physical, emotional and spiritual lives.

IT WORKS

Through the years, I have been used by God as the mentor in several people's lives. As young men have expressed their call into the ministry, I have taken them under my wings and helped guide them through the process. They would be recognized as a candidate for ordination by receiving a minister's license, and then I would develop them over the next year or so.

I would really get into their lives. Not only was I teaching them about pastoral ministry, study and preaching; but also about their personal lives, family, finances, marriage and their personal, daily walk with God. It was an exhilarating time in both of our lives, but sometimes pretty tough. I had to speak the truth in love, not just what they wanted to hear, if they were to be effective and able to succeed in their ministries.

I have had this relationship many times in my career as a pastor. It is a healthy means of feeling covered by an older and wiser minister. Now, my Bishop serves in this capacity with me. He is like a spiritual father and I lean upon him for his proven wisdom and years of experience in ministry.

GROUP

CHAPTER 6

"Where there is no counsel, the people fall; But in the multitude of counselors there is safety."

Proverbs 11:14

Another method of achieving accountability that is successful is in the use of a group. In this setting a number of individuals come together and create an encouraging environment using positive peer pressure to encourage victorious living.

Peer pressure is an extremely effective tool. We are first introduced to it usually in our teen age years. Often this follows us into our adulthood. Right or wrong, a lot of adults make home purchases, vehicle purchases and other financial decisions based on what others will think about them.

This type of influence is usually referred to in a negative sense, i.e., kids get into drugs because of peer pressure. They begin to steal or to drink for the same reason. However, in the area of accountability, the pressure is positive.

Together the group shares their experiences and weaknesses. If front of everyone they must confess their failures. This positive pressure can be a real motivating factor to keep the commitment, especially if they visualize all the faces of the group and know that they will have to explain why they failed.

Peer pressure is an extremely effective tool

AA

This type of group is the basis for the success of the Alcoholics Anonymous program that has helped an untold number of alcoholics and other addicts achieve victory over their addictions. It has proven to be effective over the decades and has become a staple in substance abuse treatment. I have met hundreds who give the positive accountability of this program credit for both getting and keeping them sober.

The group is formed around a common problem and a common goal. The problem is of course that they all struggle with alcoholism. It has taken control of their lives and in many cases is ruining their relationships and careers.

> **The group is formed around both a common problem and a common goal**

The common goal is to be set free from the addiction in order to live a productive life and have growing and meaningful relationships.

Once a person decides to face his/her alcoholism, they attend their first meeting where they announce their problem and submit to both the group and a sponsor. Between meetings, the sponsor (another person on the road to recovery) is available to help the new person on their new path.

So if they find themselves in a position of weakness and are tempted to consume alcohol, they should call their sponsor and let the sponsor help them get through the situation without "falling off the wagon" by drinking again.

The weekly meetings (many attend daily meeting or at least several per week) are a time where they are held accountable to the group as a whole as to their progress since the last meeting.

Milestones are celebrated as "chips" are given out the longer a person remains clean and victorious over their problem with alcoholism.

PSYCHOLOGY

This form has been modified by the psychological community in their group therapy sessions. The main difference being that there is a distinct leader who is trained in counseling.

There can be a wealth of knowledge and pertinent advice from the other members who may have achieved victory over your specific area(s) of need.

In a sense the entire nation of Israel was one large group accountability structure. Their laws, given by God on Mt. Sinai, kept them accountable to one another as they were encouraged to keep them and knew the punishment if they failed.

Some of the obvious drawbacks are that few people are willing to be transparent and share deep personal struggles with a group. Also, one must really know the other participants in order to feel secure that confidentiality is being maintained. If confidentiality is breached, then the entire accountability process is hurt.

WHAT IT ISN'T

That being said, it is extremely important to understand what this type of setting looks like and how it

The group must maintain its focus

functions in a person's life. An actual accountability group is not just a bunch of people in a pseudo therapy session trying to get in touch with their "inner child." Just because members of the group have watched Dr. Phil or read a book, doesn't qualify them as a therapist to deal with personal and personality issues. The purpose here is to help each person keep their commitments, not "fix" them.

It also is not simply another support group or Bible Study. Though those groups are important and necessary, the group must maintain its focus and not morph into something else.

Additionally, this group is definitely not to become a whining and/or complaining session about how unfair life is.

WHAT IT IS

A vibrant and effective accountability group would look like this:

It is a place where honesty rules

Three to five is an ideal number for the group. Any larger and it becomes too difficult for everyone to be involved in the conversation at a depth that is effective.

The group communicates beyond the superficial and casual. It's more than talking about the weather, church, hobbies or sports. They are getting together to share the truth of their lives.

It is a place where honesty rules. Members are open about their struggles and shortcomings. Honesty and transparency are both necessary and valued.

THE CRUSADERS

In my personal life the formation of group accountability happened as a byproduct of my love for music. I was part of a quartet in college that spent the summers on the road.

Our goal was to encourage other believers with gospel music and share our testimonies of how Jesus had transformed our lives.

We were active in some camp meetings and preached weekend revivals at some churches, but mostly we performed one concert after the other from town to town and state to state.

GROUP

The Crusaders quartet became my accountability group. We lived together on the road for three months out of the year. We kept each other faithful to God over many miles. This was very instrumental in developing my spiritual walk as a young college student. I thank God regularly for sending those men into my life and using them to keep me on track.

COUPLE

CHAPTER 7

"Can two walk together, unless they are agreed?"

Amos 3:3

This means of accomplishing accountability requires two sets of couples which hold each other to respective commitments.

Typically, these pertain to marriage, family, child rearing and personal relationships. This accountability relationship can be particularly helpful to those couples in parallel circumstances who share mutual experiences.

By this I mean their lives are similar. Perhaps they are both newlyweds and are working through some of the same challenges in their new marriages.

Parents of infants and toddlers are another point of mutual concern and development. The couple can hold each other accountable for their parenting skills as well as making sure that they make time for the continued development of their marriage.

Each stage of life can draw couples together. The different levels of child rearing, children in college, empty nest, grandchildren and even retirement can all produce a possible area of personal accountability that the couples can help each other through.

> **Each stage of life can draw couples together**

This form of accountability usually results in a very strong, intimate bond with the couples involved. Their friendship deepens and they develop a relationship that impacts their lives for a very long time.

I have seen couples become such good friends through this process that they are as close (even closer sometimes) than their own families.

COMBINED METHOD

Sometimes this method is combined with the Mentor method where a more mature couple helps with a newly married or newly saved couple. Then it also can add a unique Bible study feature.

A lot of churches are using this form for both pre-marital and marital counseling. Most pastors would be glad to suggest a couple that would be willing to enter into this type of arrangement.

I have seen couples become such good friends through this process

FINANCES

One of the challenging areas that couples face is in

the area of finances. The society we live in places a lot of emphasis on financial success.

Our world system puts a lot of pressure on young people to look and act the part of being successful in the eye of their peers. It can create stresses on a newly married couple to make financial decisions that are difficult to overcome. Many divorced couple site financial problems as one of the leading reasons for their marital collapse.

Many para-church ministries have been developed in order to help people through the difficulties of money management and debt relief. Books have been written on the subject and many seminars are available to attend and even view on the internet.

The couple/mentor relationship can help in this area. A mature couple can help guide the younger and inexperienced couple as they develop their financial systems.

Our educational system is very inept at teaching our young people how to manage money, budget their expenses and develop a long-term view of their financial plans.

This type of accountability can help as the new couple establishes their priorities, considers their debts, and makes strategies for their long term investments and decisions. The mentors can aid them in establishing a budget which includes tithing and saving, giving and investing, or living debt free and developing a plan for a prosperous future.

DISCIPLESHIP

In the early '80's, the church I was attending, lead by my accountability partner, Rev. David Mercer, began a discipleship program. This program was very individualistic and relied on a close bond between the participants. It worked perfectly in this couple/mentoring accountability structure.

YES, YOU CAN! YOU JUST NEED HELP

The process was intentional. The newly converted couple came to my house once a week for about three months. We took them through a program designed for new believers to help them in their new walk with Christ. It was very effective. We dealt with topics such as: knowing you are saved, attending church, prayer, tithing, temptation etc.

In that setting, the new couple could ask questions and discuss how their new walk with God was changing their lives. This change was not only as an individual, but also as a couple.

The end result of this type of discipleship structure was that the couple we worked with for those three months went on to become Christian leaders in the church. They developed their spiritual gifts and natural talents and employed them in the local church.

As an added benefit, our relationship grew extremely close and they were named the god-parents for my children. That couple has a special place in my heart and it is exciting each time I hear from one of them.

IT'S NOT EASY

This relationship, though, is usually weak in the realm of dealing with hidden weaknesses. Personal struggles are rarely revealed in the presence of more than one person and even less likely to be confessed in an environment consisting of the opposite sex.

As well, it is difficult at times for a spouse to share some weaknesses for fear of hurting their mate, especially if they have lustful, pornographic, unfaithful tendencies or actual experiences. The embarrassment of the offended spouse might be too great for that type of arraignment and the continuation of the accountability relationship might be placed at risk.

Also, if the spouse hears you make commitments that will change your relationship with them in any way, it can be easy for them to assume the role of the accountability partner 24/7 and "nag" about those commitments between accountability group sessions.

SPOUSAL

CHAPTER 8

"He who finds a wife finds a good thing, And obtains favor from the Lord."

Proverbs 18:22

This method is pretty much self-explanatory.

This is really a one-on-one accountability arrangement within boundaries of the marriage relationship. Though there are very real and evident challenges, overcoming them promises to be provide an extremely rewarding avenue in which to achieve accountability.

No one really knows you any better than your spouse. They know what you are like behind the closed doors of your home. They can tell when you are feeling great and when you are down in the dumps. They see you studying your Bible and praying. They know when you are fasting or making the decision to not watch a movie because of its content or rating.

Your partner sees how you act and how you react in about every type of situation imaginable. It is hard to hide your actions from them. Their presence is a constant reminder of your promises and commitments.

> **It is hard to hide your actions from your spouse**

Remember that when God made man, He said that it was not good for man to be alone and so He created Eve to be Adam's helpmate. What better way to assist one another than to keep each other accountable? It works both ways. Men are to keep the women accountable as well as the women helping the men.

TWO FORMS

Spousal accountability may take one of two forms:

1. Open accountability

2. Closed or specific accountability

Both forms can be extremely effective; however, care should be taken to draw distinct lines so the two do not evolve into or inhibit the other. Though both open and closed accountability can be, and some may argue possibly should be included in every method or type of accountability relationship, the distinction is must be more defined and regulated in spousal accountability.

What is the difference between open and closed accountability relationships? I am so glad that you asked this important question!

OPEN ACCOUNTABILITY

When we speak of open accountability we are referring to the scope of the areas the accountability relationship will encompass. In the open format all areas of the participants' lives and thoughts are being questioned, inspected and thoroughly examined according to their commitments.

> **Open:**
>
> **All areas of life are questioned, inspected and examined**

There is basically no area of the life that is not involved. The "openness" of the relationship allows each participant the liberty and freedom to ask whatever questions are necessary to help the other person fulfill his/her responsibilities, promises, vows and/or and obligations.

CLOSED ACCOUNTABILITY

As you might deduce, closed accountability therefore is limited or specific in its nature. It does not allow for the generic or broad brush stroke. It has a specific area in which accountability is focused and all the other areas are "closed" off from the relationship.

Closed:

Focused area of growth

The specific areas of this type of spousal accountability relationship may include areas such as; maintaining a daily devotional time, keeping a prayer journal, reducing the amount time one spends on the computer on in front of the television.

Closed accountability deals with personal goals that are measurable and can easily be viewed and determined.

This leads to a very important concept if spousal accountability is the method God chooses for you to pursue.

KNOW THE BORDERS

As you can well imagine, there can be a fine line between holding your mate accountable and "nagging."

If the accountability relationship becomes a forum for nagging, then it would begin to undermine the entire marital relationship.

In order to overcome this possible hazard, some distinct guidelines or "rules" should be honestly and purposefully put in place. The main rule should be in regards to the time of accountability.

A couple would need to set a time for a weekly or bi-weekly accountability meeting.

It cannot be an "any time you like it" mentality. In other words it shouldn't happen when you are watching TV, passing each other in the hallway, or lying in bed at night.

If certain guidelines are established and adhered to faithfully, then this method could deepen your marital communication and strengthen your overall marital relationship. Face it; no one should be more concerned for your spiritual and personal well-being than your spouse.

For some it might be best if they began this type of accountability as a "closed" or specific method until the borders are established and the spouses become accustomed to living with their accountability partner.

YES, YOU CAN! YOU JUST NEED HELP

<u>MY WIFE</u>

Kim, my wife, is an excellent accountability partner. She understands the borders. She knows the areas that can drag me down. She is also very aware of the temptations with which the world attacks men.

In order that there be no impropriety or darkness allowed into our ministry, she has full permission and access to my computers and emails. There can be no conversations that she is not aware of that are taking place through electronic means. She knows all the passwords to my accounts. She can look at my computer at any time to assure that I have not crossed the line in viewing sexually inappropriate sites. She even has access to my voice mail so that nothing can be done out of order.

"Wow," you may say, "that's a little too much." Not for us. Our relationship is THAT critical. How can we minister if we allow a foothold in our life? Our purity is THAT important! Any hint of sexual indiscretion can ruin what God has destined that we do for Him and our witness to the world.

MUTUAL,
ONE-ON-ONE

CHAPTER 9

"Then the Lord said to Cain, 'Where is Abel your brother?' He said, 'I do not know. Am I my brother's keeper?'"

Genesis 4:9

In this scenario, two people hold each other mutually accountable. This is probably the most common form of accountability and is what is usually thought of when the topic is discussed.

The two partners meet regularly to review each other's faithfulness to keep their commitments. They consistently pray for one another and keep all items confidential.

Since there are only two individuals involved, they should be of the same sex so as to avoid any emotional pitfall.

YES, YOU CAN! YOU JUST NEED HELP

This is very effective if approached with the proper motives. The two partners are usually on about the same plain both spiritually and emotionally. Often they have a lot in common such as their marital status and age.

Because of these similarities, they often face some of the same temptations, problems, and challenges.

An added benefit is that the two will more than likely become very good friends. Remember, friendship is based on trust and these partners will trust each other with their personal struggles and intimate thoughts.

> **This is probably the most common form of accountability**

Care should be taken to not just let these meetings together become a catch up time on work, the family, and life in general, but also make sure that your keep it on target. You are there for a reason, and that is to help each other stay focused on living a life of integrity. Often, God will not lead you to your best friend as a partner, but will use this as a means to develop a new relationship in your life based on this common goal. In a lot of ways that is good. I have had my best friends as accountability partners in the past. It is too easy to pull the wool over their eyes and divert the conversation if you have had some problems since you last met.

RESPONSIBILITY

The word, "responsibility" is a compound word. That is, it is made of two words put together. In this case the two words are:

Respond and Ability.

Even as far back as in the story of Cain and Able, God requires that we are to be our brother's keeper. I believe from the Scriptures a case can be made that God wants to help us develop the "ability" to "respond" in a redemptive way to the things that we find when we locate our brother in the Lord.

Mutual, one-on-one accountability means that I have become personally responsible for your growth and you have become personally responsible for mine. We both give each other the right to ask one another anything in our lives, to meddle in our affairs and to mind each other's business. This permission opens doors to find out the real underlying "root" of the problem on bearing bad "fruit.

INSTRUCTION AND CORRECTION

Most of us shrink back from allowing a peer to give us instruction or correction. But the Scriptures have something to say about our response in Proverbs 10:17,

"He who keeps instruction is in the way of life,
But he who refuses correction goes astray."

We must come to see how God uses correction to bless our lives.

The Hebrew word translated "instruction" is "muwcar" which means a verbal chastening that serves as a warning against actual damage.

Correction, or as is translated in other versions as "reproof", is taken from the Hebrew word "Towkechah" which entails the meaning of a rebuke designed to bring correction to some aspect of your life.

So instruction serves as a warning and reproof as a solution. Apply those definitions as you read the following passages from the Scriptures.

Proverbs 12:1,
"Whoever loves instruction loves

knowledge, But he who hates correction is
stupid.

Proverbs 15:5,
"A fool despises his father's instruction, But
he who receives correction is prudent."

Proverbs 15: 10,
"Harsh discipline is for him who forsakes
the way, and he who hates correction will
die."

Proverbs 15:31-32,
"The ear that hears the rebukes of life will
abide among the wise.
He who disdains instruction despises his
own soul,
But he who heed rebuke gets understanding."

Basically what is being said in plain terms is, if you forsake correction, you go astray. If you avoid it, you are stupid. If you presume that you don't need it, you will end up in strife and if you hate it, you will die. Strong terms I know, God must think it is pretty important. I know, we'd rather skip those sections and move on to what makes us feel better. Keep reading.

But if you receive it, there will be wisdom and honor; you will be prudent, you will come into knowledge, you will be on the path of life, it is a sign of friendship, it's a means to learning wisdom and it is a medicine.

CONSIDER THIS

If you are going to be used by God to give correction and direction in your partner's life, you must be willing to receive the same! It is mutual, not one-sided correction. You must humble yourself to accept as well as to give.

Understand that in giving reproof very often you will see in others things that are a reflection of yourself. It is sometimes like looking into a mirror. You may very well reprove yourself as well as your accountability partner!

Be aware of assuming the attitude that reproving others is a gift or calling. It is not listed as either in the Scriptures. No one has the right or authority to just walk through the body reproving people. It is not a "ministry" office in the church. In other words, correct when necessary within the boundaries of the accountability relationship, otherwise keep your nose out of what isn't your business in someone else's life. Remember that the Apostle Paul gives the overall attitude we must have in this type of situation,

> **You must humble yourself to accept as well as to give**

MUTUAL, ONE-ON-ONE

Ephesians 4:15

"but, the speaking the truth in love,
may grow up in all things into Him who is
the head – Christ"

Sincere love has to be established before we begin to correct or reprove. And I would say that the more severe the rebuke, the deeper the love. If we haven't built someone up, and loved them with the "Agape" love of God, then we have no business tearing them down.

As we must instruct and correct each other, we must learn to use Wisdom.

Proverbs 25:11-12,

"A word fitly spoken is like apples of gold in
settings of silver. Like an earring of gold
and an ornament of
fine gold is a wise rebuker to an obedient
ear."

Proverbs 15:2,

"The tongue of the wise uses knowledge rightly, But the mouth of fools pours forth foolishness."

Lastly, remain patient. The Scriptures also remind us in Proverbs 28:23,

Remain Patient

"He who rebukes a man will find more favor afterward than he who flatters with the tongue."

MORE THAN THAT

I understand that we have spent a lot of time

looking at instruction and correction. I realize also that this is not the only important part of keeping each other accountable. However, it is often the area that is over looked or missing in accountability relationships that have failed.

There must be godly love as well as times of joyful celebration. We must be patient, kind and gentle. We also must stay at peace with one another and yet faithful to our mission.

HOW TO GET STARTED

CHAPTER 10

*"In all your ways acknowledge Him,
And He shall direct your paths. Do not be wise
in your own eyes; Fear the LORD and depart from
evil."*

Proverbs 3:6-7

All of this information is good to think about and consider, but how does one act upon the information? How do we get started on this journey of being held accountable?

REMEMBER TOM?

Our friend Tom from the earlier pages of the book needs to develop some type of accountability structure in his life. Let's walk through this process with him.

Tom, if you remember, has over extended his time between his family, his church and his work. Counting on his new position and salary increase, he also had over extended his finances by adding a car payment and an insurance policy to the family budget.

Realizing that he is beginning to sink under the pressure, Tom picks up a book much like this and realizes he is missing the structure and focus that an accountability relationship will help him attain.

TIME TO TALK
TO GOD

Tom understands that the first step in establishing a successful accountability relationship is to seek God's guidance. He knows that he must go before his heavenly Father in prayer and ask for Him to honor His Word which promises that He will direct our paths if we lean not unto our own understanding and acknowledge Him. (Prov. 3:6-7)

As he lifts this matter up to his heavenly Father, he realizes that he is seeking guidance on two very specific things.

1) Which method of accountability should he use? (Mentor, couple, etc.)

2) Who should be his accountability partner?

Do Not Underestimate this step.

Tom must not underestimate this step. This should not be a ritual, or an obligatory exercise. It should be a time of focused prayer and discernment of God's direction in the selection of this extremely important method and partner in his spiritual walk.

After some thought and prayer, he decides he should go through the Word of God in his private time and carefully examine other accountability relationships and see what the Spirit says through His Word.

Mutual, one-on-one, accountability is the method that stirs his heart. He accepts that God has spoken to him and he decides to step out in faith and begin this process. How does he begin? More prayer and time with God! Now he has to choose a partner with God's help.

Understand that God may have someone entirely different than what Tom's mind suggests. He must put his own understanding of this behind him and seek his Father's direction.

Some practical suggestions Tom keeps in mind are:

1. Another man. Real accountability can create emotional ties with someone of the opposite sex. Just the concept of meeting with another woman once a week to share his struggles makes Tom aware of the potential pitfalls.

2. He is looking for another man who is sincere about growing as a Christian and will take this commitment seriously.

3. Tom is also looking at people he actually enjoys spending time with and they like each other.

4. He is looking for a peer; someone who is his "equal," and who is not impressed by Tom.

5. And lastly, someone he respects, and with whom he can build solid trust. He is keeping in mind that, over time, he will share many aspects of his life with this person.

After prayerfully seeking God's direction, Tom makes a list of seven names of people who he thinks God is telling him would make a good reliable partner.

He uses the form in the appendix at the back of this book to make his list. Next, he again prays over that list for a week and then puts the list aside for a week. He then goes back to it and prays over the list of potential partner again.

YES, YOU CAN! YOU JUST NEED HELP

Tom's next step is to number those on his list in the order in which he believes God is directing him to approach them.

APPROACHING
POTENTIAL PARTNERS

Once the Holy Spirit has made it clear to Tom how to order his list of potential of accountability partners, HE must take the next step. TOM must make the break from his comfort zone and approach the number one person on his list.

Nothing will happen from this point on if HE do not stretch himself and make the first move. He must take charge of his attitude and step out in faith that God has directed him into this and has given him the names to call.

HOW TO GET STARTED

He must not wait any longer!!

He should not prolong the first contact. He has to just jump in and do it and watch God do the rest.

When approaching the person Tom must remember to:

1. Explain the purpose and plan of accountability. He gives them a copy of this book as a guide to explain the reason he feels that an accountability relationship would be good and proper for the two of them.

2. Clearly outline his expectation of a partner and suggest a few days of prayerful consideration before being given an answer as to whether or not they will join him on this quest. He makes it known that he has prayed and that God has laid them upon his heart as a potential partner. However, Tom is wise enough to understand he should not use that as an attempt to force them into the relationship. This must continue to be led by the Holy Spirit of God.

3. Understand that the first few on his list may say, "NO." But that is O.K. He keeps asking until he has the one that understands his heart and is willing to help him. As it turns out, it is not Tom's best friend.

4. Tom keeps in mind that if his potential partner has some reservations, but is interested in the concept, then he should consider them as a possibility. He knows that the first meeting will be a foundational meeting anyway and may help them to make their decision in a more informed way.

TIME TO MEET

Tom has found a willing partner, Jerry! He is one of the young business men in his church with a family much like his own. They actually were on the same golf team at the church's last tournament.

As soon as they agreed together to form this

partnership, they **begin at once** to set up the first meeting! Since Jerry is definite in his commitment to accountability with Tom, a meeting schedule is established. They decide they will meet every week.

They agree that this gives a space of time between their meetings, doesn't cause a bottleneck in their schedules, and yet is close enough to help catch one another if one of them has begun to fall since the last meeting.

Next they set the time limit for the meeting at one hour. About twenty five minutes will be spent on each person and five minutes will be dedicated to prayer for that partner.

It is critical that they don't allow a lot of time to slide by, so they jump right in and set the first appointment so that they can get the "ball rolling." (The sooner you do the same, the sooner you will begin experiencing the wonderful victory that can and will be yours!)

This is where the line is drawn in the sand.

YES, YOU CAN! YOU JUST NEED HELP

Here is where these two men actually determine to become persons of integrity. It doesn't happen just because they read a book or make a few calls. They could have gone through the process up until this point and still avoided getting serious about keeping the commitment.

Once Tom and Jerry physically meet for the first time with one another, they have laid the first brick in the wall of victory in their spiritual quest to build a life of integrity.

Begin

At

Once!

THE FIRST MEETING

CHAPTER 11

"but, speaking the truth in love, may grow up in all things into Him who is the head—Christ"

Ephesians 4:15

Now that Tom and Jerry are face to face with their new accountability partner, "What do they do?"

First of all, they set each other at ease with a vow of confidentiality. NOTHING that is shared in the bond of accountability should be shared with others.

A breach of this kind could undermine the success of their partnership and possibly destroy their friendship as well. They use the *Accountability Commitment* form in Appendix C as a pattern for their commitment to each other.

Next, Tom (the person who initiated this partnership)

breaks the ice and begins sharing. He asks his new friend to question him at each meeting on how he has kept his commitments.

After overcoming the initial awkwardness and the fear of sharing, Jerry has an opportunity to be candid with Tom regarding his areas of weakness.

An important part of this process is that they be sincerely open with one another. It will do little good have these meetings if they both sidestep the deep issues of their life. If either one of them hides behind superficial issues, they are only strengthening the stronghold of deception that they have built around themselves.

Since they were a little unsure how to begin, they decided to look over the list of possible questions in Appendix E. There seemed to be some areas they wanted to cover from that list, so they used those questions. Some of their specific weaknesses were not listed, so they used the format of that list to help them formulate their own.

The important aspect here is that they begin by putting forth a sincere effort to deal with their real weaknesses. It may be that some of their more comfortable ones will surface during the first few meetings and that the deeper ones will be revealed after they have established the new partnership over a length of time.

LET'S MAKE A LIST

Now that they have started to share from their hearts with one another, they take the time to put the issue(s) in form of a written question.

Since they are meeting every week, they may have a tendency to forget the details of their partner's goals and commitments and therefore not ask the proper questions. This type of proper documentation will provide Tom and Jerry with the necessary information to be effective accountability partners.

As with Tom and Jerry, it will be helpful to develop your own list of questions pertaining to frequent problem areas that your partner can use to begin with. Again, as a guide, us the comprehensive list included in Appendix E. In this way you know how to adequately question your partner in the next meeting. You will also know how your friend will be questioning you. It is possible that you even share the same areas of concern and can benefit from one another.

Documentation, like this, is an essential part of the relationship. You will do your partner little good if you forget what you should hold him accountable for, and vice-versa.

THE GROWING LIST

This should be an on-going list. It may be altered as frequently as each meeting, but never remove any items from the list. Keep them there so that periodically you will be reminded to revisit that area so that your friend does not get slack in the area and fail to report it to you.

It is most advantageous to keep a notebook in which you document the questions and the responses. The notebook can also help you pray for your accountability partner during the time between meetings and provide them with a praise note when they have overcome in an area.

INSIST ON SENCERITY

Next, in order for this process to truly have the intended effect on their lives, Tom and Jerry must be sincere. They must have a purpose and keep their meeting designed to accomplish that purpose. What they do not need is someone else to justify or condone their failures.

Accountability is not about comfort and consolation for missing our goal. It is about having someone whose opinions we value lovingly rebuke us for not being faithful to God, others and ourselves.

Though you will no doubt develop a close relationship with your accountability partner, at your meetings you must maintain a sincere, tough-love attitude toward what you are doing.

TOUGH LOVE

Paul Borthwick in his book, _"Leading the Way"_ makes the following observation:

> _"But too often we confuse love with permissiveness. It is not love to fail to dissuade another believer from sin any more than it is love to fail to take a drink away from an alcoholic or matches away from a baby. True fellowship out of love for one another demands accountability."_

For example, if your partner admits he has not had his daily time with God since you last met because he has been too busy, your reaction should NOT be, "I understand where you are coming from. I'm a busy person as well and sometimes have a hard time fitting my private time in. Let's try to do better next week."

This type of response would allow an attitude of permissiveness into your relationship and your partner would soon loose respect for your opinion and suggestions. It does not reflect a sincere concern for your partner. You have accepted the responsibility of helping them keep their commitments, not justifying their failures.

Instead your reaction should be more like this, "It really disturbs me to hear that you have not kept your commitment to God to have a regular time alone with Him each day. You know as well as I do that this is your most important appointment of the day. No other event on your schedule is as important as your time alone with

Almighty God. Today you should repent of your failure and renew your vow to God. Take a long look at your schedule and consider your time with God as a daily standing appointment that cannot be broken."

With a spirit of love, yet toughness and earnestness, your job as an accountability partner is to call sin . . . Sin and failure—Failure. Lead your friend to repentance and renewal of his commitment. "Letting it slide," could undermine both his commitment and the integrity of your accountability relationship. Don't accept or give excuses. Stay true to what you are trying to accomplish here.

KEEP THE
STANDARD HIGH

If you lower the standard by "letting him slide," then he will perform at this new, lower standard also. The end result will be that he justifies your failures in return and you are not challenged or motivated to really change.

Keep the standard high. Be firm. Don't allow for lame excuses. Hold your partner to his/her word and make them see that they have disappointed you by their failure. Don't consent to lowering the bar of excellence.

After you have lovingly rebuked sin and failure and led them to repentance, become their best cheer leader. Help to find ways that they can accomplish their goal and speak life into them. Believe in them and let them know it.

WHAT'S NEXT?

CHAPTER 12

"But if we walk in the light as He is in the light, we have fellowship with one another, and the blood of Jesus Christ His Son cleanses us from all sin."

1 John 1:7

The bottom line result is that you WILL begin experiencing VICTORY in areas that you once failed in!!!!

Walking with God will be more enthusiastic. You will be planting the seed within you of a positive attitude toward your ability to keep your commitments. Life will be full of victories in the areas that have long given you pain and sorrow.

You will change the cycle from one of defeat to one of Victory!!! YOU WILL!!

TESTIFY TO VICTORIES!

Having experienced these victories, we must be faithful to God to testify to His power in our lives and let the world know how wonderful it is to be walking in victory with God every day.

Your testimony may be what is needed for God to begin a work of conviction in the life of someone else and bring them into a right relationship with Almighty God.

BEGIN NOW!

THE WORST THING YOU CAN DO with the information in this booklet is to read the pages; then lay it down and do nothing.

If you are sincere in your walk with God, if you desire to be a person of integrity, if you have a deep heart-felt desire to keep your commitments, then begin **NOW!!**

It bears repeating: **<u>BEGIN NOW!!!!!</u>**

Before you lay down this book, think of the names of some people who could possibly become an accountability partner. Turn to Appendix A and follow the outline of the steps to begin your accountability partnership.

May God bless you and give you the courage and power to start your cycle of Victory NOW!!!

<u>WHY DO PEOPLE AVOID ACCOUNTABILITY?</u>

After reading through this material and seeing the possibilities, what would prevent someone from establishing an accountability relationship? I mean there must be something that causes them to draw back from the potential victory they could experience. In my experience there are at least seven different areas that will prevent people from making this crucial step:

1. Fear of the Unknown
2. Fear of Exposure
3. Fear of Rejection
4. Ignorance
5. Bondage
6. Motivation
7. Pride

Let's take the time to examine these areas. Perhaps we can determine what has been keeping us from entering into accountability.

FEAR OF THE UNKOWN

Fear is powerful. Fear can cause us to think and behave irrationally. It can be a debilitating force. I have been incapacitated by fear in my life.

I attended a Christian boarding school in the late 1970's. The high school was located in the Appalachian

Mountains and there was not a lot for teenagers to do in those hills.

One Sunday afternoon a group of young men and I decided to hike through the woods and into the creek. There was a "cut-away" near the creek. A cut-away is a section of mountain where the natural incline of the hill had been cut back to allow for a road to be put in its place.

This particular cut-away was very tall and straight up. Someone, I don't remember who, had the bright idea of scaling this cut-away. I sat in shock as everyone agreed that this was a "great" idea.

Oh, did I mention that I do not like heights?

I watched as everyone slowly ascended the hillside. Using little rocks and twigs, holes and dirt to create some type of foothold to continue their climb. My heart began to race as one after the other made the commitment to go up. I knew that I would eventually have to climb as well.

YES, YOU CAN! YOU JUST NEED HELP

Finally, everyone one was at the top and I was left at the bottom. I began my ascent. Slowly and carefully I tried to follow where my friends had placed their hands and feet.

About half way up the rock face, my arms and legs began to shake uncontrollably. My blood pressure must have sky-rocketed because all I could hear was my heart beating in my head. I couldn't look down. I couldn't look up. So I just stopped where I was. I couldn't move either way.

My friends tried to coach me. They told me where to place my hands and feet. The encouraged me to keep moving. But I could not let go of my position and would not even try to move.

Finally, my best childhood friend climbed down the cut-away to my position and physically took me the rest of the way to the top.

When one doesn't know what to expect from a new relationship such as accountability, there may be some fear associated with what is unknown. Many questions may arise and without proper answers, the fear may even seem warranted. Next we will deal with specific areas where fear could act as a deterrent to moving forward in an accountability partnership.

FEAR OF EXPOSURE

When a person understands the real purpose of an effective accountability relationship, it can be overwhelming. Extremely so!

As they comprehend how transparent they will have to be in order for it to be a successful arraignment some people freeze in fear like I froze on the cut-away.

The very idea that they will become vulnerable to another human being causes them to stop in their tracks. Someone else will know their short-comings. Another person will know their secrets . . . their sins.

Rather than exposing their faults, they will tighten their grip and dig into their foothold and stay right where they are. They will not risk revealing anything because of fear.

FEAR OF REJECTION

Closely related to the phobia of exposure is the fear rejection. Part of why someone is unwilling to expose their weaknesses is shame or maybe pride. Another reason is that they are unsure how the other person will react once they know the real problem(s) they are facing.

"What if they don't like me anymore" runs through their mind. "Maybe they will think I'm just a poor excuse for a Christian."

Rather than risk that rejection, many people will just make the decision to not get involved in a real, life altering accountability relationship.

IGNORANCE

Some people are not involved in a relationship like this just because they don't truly understand the need for it. They have not been taught the power that is associated with a vibrant and effective accountability partnership.

Often people will not get involved in those things that they do not understand. Having read this far into this book, I can't see how this could be your excuse any longer.

BONDAGE

Through our continual practice of deceit and sin, Satan can begin to develop a foothold of bondage in a person's life and spirit. Realizing that this type of accountability relationship will expose and help a person seek deliverance from bondage will sometimes cause them to run away from getting involved.

Physically, spiritually, and emotionally we can be bound and not even realize the depth to which we are attached to our sins. Secret sins especially have a strong grip on the soul. This type of partnership, if we are honest and true in our efforts to make it work, will shine the light upon those dark areas of our life.

I grew up in southern Georgia. Now, it seemed no matter how clean you were and no matter how often you had the pest control experts at your house, there were always going to be roaches around. I mean the big, black, scary kind. They are mainly nocturnal. If you had any roaches, they were sure to come out at night. If you got up in the middle of the night for a glass of water and turned the light on in the kitchen, you would invariably see those creatures scurrying across the floor, cabinets, and walls to find a place to hide from the light.

WHAT'S NEXT?

Just like those big, black, and nocturnal southern roaches reacted when a light was turned on, so will those who are in bondage once the light of God's Spirit shines over their sins.

Bondage is darkness. The only way out of the darkness is to walk into the light. The Apostle John encourages us in his first epistle by saying in chapter one verses 5-7,

"This is the message which we have heard from Him and declare to you, that God is light and in Him is no darkness at all. If we say that we have fellowship with Him, and walk in darkness, we lie and do not practice the truth.

But if we walk in the light as He is in the light, we have fellowship with one another, and the blood of Jesus Christ His Son cleanses us from all sin."

MOTIVATION

There can often be a problem of perception that keeps people from being motivated to enter into accountability relationships. That perception may be that their current situation is not critical enough yet to motivate them to change.

Often we are not willing to make changes because change is difficult. A lot of us are only willing to change when the pain or difficulty of staying where we are is greater than the pain of changing. We choose the lesser of the two.

Because of this tendency, we may wait until we hit "rock bottom" before we change. We hold on, scratching and fighting to do it ourselves until the weight of the problems and commitments is too great to continue so we cry out for help.

The reality is that if we will be proactive and utilize the tool of accountability before being totally overwhelmed, we may avoid that all together. We may find that through our accountability relationship there is a way to stem the tide of waves that are crashing in on us.

PRIDE

A final reason I see that would keep someone from engaging in this accountability partnership is that of pride. A person's pride may cause him/her to be unable to see or understand their personal need for accountability.

The irony of the situation is that the very existence of pride of this magnitude is actually a reason to get help through accountability. The partnership established can help deal with the pride that can destroy a person. Most of us have at least heard, if not quoted part of Proverbs 16:18,

YES, YOU CAN! YOU JUST NEED HELP

*"Pride goes before destruction and a haughty
spirit before a fall."*

Proverbs 29:23 continues the thought by saying,
*"A man's pride will bring him low, but the
humble in spirit will retain honor."*

Jesus was teaching one day and he spoke concerning the things that will defile a man. In Mark's seventh chapter there are four verses where Jesus creates a list of things which come from within a person and defile. Most of the list is ugly, glaring, egregious sins, and then our Lord throws pride right in the middle of those awful things. Mark 7:20-23,

*"And He said, "What comes out of a man,
that defiles a man.
For from within, out of the heart of men,
proceed evil thoughts, adulteries,*

fornications, murders,
thefts, covetousness, wickedness, deceit,
lewdness, an evil eye, blasphemy, pride,
foolishness.
All these evil things come from within and
defile a man."

The person who thinks that he/she has arrived and so mature in the spiritual walk that they do not need assistance with their growth is one who is allowing pride to cover their need. We all need to learn to walk in the grace of God and we need His grace to cover our mistakes, short-comings and sins. Pride does not lead to the path of grace, but it leads to being resisted by God Himself. Listen to what the Apostle Peter said in 1 Peter 5:5 as he quotes from Proverbs 3:34,

"God resists the proud,
but gives grace to the humble."

YES, YOU CAN! YOU JUST NEED HELP

Most of us do not like to realize the truth that pride is actually the original sin of the angel Lucifer. He was proud of himself. He was proud of his position. He had great pride in his looks and abilities. He thought his great power was enough to unseat the King of the Universe and overthrow His kingdom.

What arrogance! What pride!!

When we act or react in pride, we are more like Satan. When we walk in humility we are more like our Lord, Jesus (Phil 2).

FINAL WORDS

What are you going to do now? Are you going to accept one of these excuses or some other explanation of why you shouldn't submit yourself to an accountability relationship?

WHAT'S NEXT?

Or are you going to walk in faith and find the right method and partner(s) God has for you and begin to actually make some real measurable strides in your desire to walk in integrity and grow spiritually?

It's now up to you. The ball, as they say, is in your court. You can now close this book and place it on your book shelf and make a mental (prideful) note that you have finished another one, or you can dissect your life and make the truths you have read a reality in your personal life.

I encourage you to take the next step. Be a leader. Take charge of your life.

Stop allowing others and circumstances to push you into their mold. Put on God as a living sacrifice and use the methods of accountability to live a life of worship to Him.

APPENDIX

APPENDIX A

STEPS TO BEGIN A SUCCESSFUL
ACCOUNTABILITY PARTNERSHIP

1. Seek God for the type of accountability relationship to start

2. Seek God for a partner

3. List 7 names of potential partners

4. Pray through the list

5. Place the names in the order you will ask them

6. Begin approaching the people in the order listed

7. Give them time to seek God

8. When a person says yes, set the first meeting

9. Commit to confidentiality (see Appendix C)

10. Be truthful and open

11. Be sincere. Don't let it slide

12. Begin praising God for Victories!!.

APPENDIX B

TYPES OF ACCOUNTABILITY
RELATIONSHIPS

MENTOR: Submitting to an older or more mature person. Receive guidance from one who has experienced victory. It can be tough having someone over you.

GROUP: More than two create positive peer pressure. One sees they are not the only struggling. It can be difficult to be intimate or open in a large group.

SPOUSAL: One to one with your spouse. No one should want you to succeed more than your spouse. It can turn into permission to nag.

MUTUAL: Two partners agree to hold one another accountable. They work together and develop trust. Can turn into a hang our session with no real focus on change.

APPENDIX C

MY LIST OF POSSIBLE
ACCOUNTABILITY PARTNERS

1. _____

2. _____

3. _____

4. _____

5. _____

6. _____

7. _____

APPENDIX D

ACCOUNTABILITY COMMITMENT

Aware of our need to meet with someone on a regular basis to check on our spiritual progress, we promise to be faithful to encourage and rebuke each other in love, and to keep all issues confidential.

Signed: _____

Signed: _____

Date: _____

ACCOUNTABILITY COMMITMENT

Aware of our need to meet with someone on a regular basis to check on our spiritual progress, we promise to be faithful to encourage and rebuke each other in love, and to keep all issues confidential.

Signed: _____

Signed: _____

Date: _____

APPENDIX E

75 SPECIFIC QUESTIONS FOR ACCOUNTABILITY

Credit Keith Drury

1. Have you had your daily time alone with God since we last met?
2. Have you taken any days alone with God?
3. Have your thoughts been pure and free from lust?
4. Have you dated your spouse every week?
5. Have you taken a day off each week?
6. Have you had a daily sharing time with your spouse?
7. Is there anyone against whom you are holding a grudge?
8. Is there any emotional attachment with someone of the opposite sex which could develop dangerously?

9. With whom could such an attachment develop in the future?

10. Have you given unselfishly to your mate's needs?

11. Are there any unresolved conflicts with your mate?

12. Have you been harsh or unkind in the use of your tongue?

13. How often have you had family altar since we last met?

14. How often have you shared your faith? When? What happened?

15. How much time have you spent with your children? Doing what?

16. Have you spread falsehoods about another (slander)?

17. Have you spread hurtful truth about another (gossip)?

18. Do you have any unmade restitutions?

19. Are you discipling your child? Mate? How? When?

20. Is your practice of keeping a journal up to date?

21. How much have you fasted since we last met?

22. Have you had nightly prayers with your spouse?

23. Report on your memorizing and meditating on Scripture.

24. How are your improving your relationship with your mate?

25. Is there a brother you should try to restore from sin?

26. When did you last give a thoughtful gift to your mate?

27. In what ways have you been tempted to be proud?

28. How have you given to the needy since we last met?

29. How much time have you wasted watching TV?

30. What about questionable movies, magazines or videos?

31. Are you completely out of installment debt?

32. How are you avoiding materialism?

33. Have you exaggerated or lied since we last met?

34. Have you been able to ignore carnal, complaining, petty people?

35. What spiritual growth books have you read since we met?

36. Of what are you afraid? How will you defy this fear?

37. How have you played "Team Ball" with others since we last met?

38. Have you had a critical spirit since we last met?

39. In what special ways have you shown love to your mate?

40. Have you been fully submissive to authority?

41. Who is it that you are tempted to envy or be jealous of?

42. Is there any believer with whom you are out of harmony?

43. Was there a time when your love for God was hotter?

44. Who are you discipling and mentoring? How?

45. How have you attempted to make peace between others?

46. Have you taken anything not belonging to you, large or small?

47. What sexual sin have you been most tempted to commit?

48. Have you a practice which may be a stumbling block to others?

49. Have you avoided outbursts of anger or rage?

50. About what have you bee inclined to boast?

51. Have you been tempted to give up? Why?

52. How have you clarified your life's mission since we last met?

53. Have you avoided fighting, quarreling, dissension and factions?

54. How have you shown enduring patience since we last met?

55. Have you avoided obscenity, foolish talk, and course jokes?

56. In what ways have you been tempted to greed?

57. Have you selfish ambition? How pure is your desire to achieve?

58. Is there hate, malice, or ill will in your heart for anyone?

59. Is there any sin, inward or outward, which has dominion over you so that you are habitually falling in this area?

60. How have you shown thanks to God and others?

61. How have you shown submission and respect to your husband?

62. How have you shown love and tenderness to your wife?

63. Have you frivolously wasted words since we last met?

64. Have you participated in fruitless arguments?

65. Do you have a teachable spirit?

66. Have you shown favoritism toward the rich or powerful? How?

67. In what way have you launched out in faith since we last met?

68. Have you abused your power over others?

69. Have you deceitfully manipulated people for your own benefit?

70. Have you been guilty of worry, anxiety or distrust of God?

71. In what ways have you shown brotherly kindness?

72. Is there any sin of another which you have come to tolerate?

73. Have you sought opportunities to serve, listen and help?

74. How have you cared for the needy since we last met?

75. To whom did you show Christ's love since we last met? How?

Also Available On Amazon.com

DR. LONNIE E. RILEY

THE EXTRAORDINARY POWER OF 1%

40 Motivational Studies
That Can Change Your Life
1% At A Time.

COMING SOON

$12.95

A four week devotional for couples.

Develop better communication as you deepen your love for one another.

WHAT'S *LOVE* GOT TO DO WITH IT?

DR. LONNIE E. RILEY

$17.95

Saving money on fInal expenses and uncovering abuses in the funeral industry.

The Final

RIP

Off

DR. LONNIE E. RILEY

SCHEDULE

DR. & MRS. RILEY

FOR YOUR EVENTS

Dr. Riley is open for scheduling for the

following events:

➢ Book Signings

➢ Speaking engagements for your
group/congregation

➢ Concerts

For information on scheduling visit

www.fmintl.org

ABOUT THE AUTHOR

Dr. Lonnie E. Riley is the Executive Director of Freedom Ministries International. He is a prolific author, song writer and teacher.

The scope of his ministry includes church planting (5 congregations), Senior and Associate pastorates, evangelist, author, and teacher.

His family consists of his wife, Kimberly and 3 grown sons; Jason (wife Kymberly), Joshua, and Randall.

The Rileys presently make their home in Myrtle Beach, SC.

www.ingramcontent.com/pod-product-compliance
Lightning Source LLC
Chambersburg PA
CBHW051956090426
42741CB00008B/1424